A Tale of ANTARCTICA

written and illustrated by
Ulco Glimmerveen

Ashton Scholastic
Auckland Sydney New York London Toronto

Evening settles on Antarctica. The low, setting sun slides past the blue mountains of ice and frozen rock. The wind has dropped to a rare calm, and the snow lies as a glistening cloak over the frozen land.

Beneath this blue and white blanket a thousand hearts lie beating, waiting . . . .

Eventually, one smart penguin lifts his head, then a second one, until finally hundreds of penguins shake off the white mantle that the storms have laid upon them. There are small ones and large ones, skinny ones and fat ones. There are quiet ones and noisy ones, silly ones and solemn ones. One of them is called Papa.

Relieved to be in fresh air again, they chatter. They haven't seen each other for days and the still air is full of noise. Their cheerful voices only begin to fade when the midnight sun hesitates above the horizon before again climbing the skies.

The penguins close their eyes and doze. Papa dreams of chasing tasty little fish in the icy depths of the polar sea, but his dream is confusing and his sleep disturbed.

Perhaps it is because spring has come to Antarctica — the time between the long, black winter and the summer when the sun doesn't set. An unsettled time, when things tend to change.

With his belly full of fish, Papa swims back to the shore, pops out of the water onto the stony beach as he has done so many times before, and waddles towards his colony.

But who is that?

Is that a huge penguin standing among his friends?

Papa is not afraid. Instead he hurries across the pebble beach, stumbling over rocks and obstacles he has never noticed before, to greet the stranger.

The stranger is large; larger than any penguin Papa has ever met. He speaks a gentle but unknown language and strokes Papa's head.

Papa is glad to make a new friend.

The spring is beautiful this year, full of promise and vibrant color. Papa and the other penguins gradually become used to the strange people who have come with Papa's friend. They do the birds no harm.

11

One afternoon, after a day of fishing in the ocean, Papa returns to the beach. He is about
pop out of the water when he discovers his favorite landing spot is covered with oil drums
boxes.

Papa is dismayed as he trudges toward his colony. The new people have littered the beach with garbage.

Instead of stroking the penguins' heads and talking nicely to them as Papa's friend does, these people have brought roaring machines that shovel away the penguins and the rocks on which they make their nests.

Papa is relieved to see Mama again, safe and sound near two of her friends. She stands very still because on her large pink feet she carries a huge egg, which she warms in the folds of her fat belly.

The egg is due to hatch very soon, and Mama and Papa are excited and happy.

Early one morning the little chick breaks away the shell and stumbles out of the egg. It looks at the world for the very first time, stretches, and demands meal after meal from its delighted parents.

Papa has noticed that the fish are not so plentiful and taste a little strange since the arrival of the people. Mama and he need to work very hard to get their chick the best of everything.

The curious chick grows and grows and demands more and more food every day.

Papa is always pleased when it's his turn to go fishing for the fast-growing chick. He like to race through the water and explore the mysterious, deep ocean.

It's wonderful fishing under the gigantic icebergs, where Papa can find thousands of krill. They are easy to catch but very small.

Papa is busy for a long time and, in his concentration, he doesn't notice the hungry leopard seal. It lurks in a gloomy crevice and suddenly shoots forward, grabbing one of Papa's companions for a meal.

Instantly, Papa forgets about the krill and rushes back to the surface.

Another shock awaits him. A thick layer of crude oil covers the waves and immediately sticks to Papa's delicate feathers. With every dive he picks up a heavier coat of oil.

It takes a great effort for Papa to reach the pebble beach and struggle ashore. Dripping with oil, Papa returns to the colony where all the chicks are huddled together in large groups. He is greeted enthusiastically by Junior and Mama, but they soon realize the danger Papa is in.

Mama rushes to get help. She climbs over the piles of garbage to the shelters of the people.

Everyone ignores her desperate pleas for attention until she reaches the shelter where Papa's friend lives. He dresses up to face the bitter cold and follows Mama outside. When he discovers what has happened to Papa, his speech no longer sounds gentle. Followed by Mama, Junior, and some curious neighbors, Papa is carried to the base.

Papa gets very special treatment with powdered clay to absorb the oil and, although it makes him look very peculiar, the penguins have confidence in their friend's wisdom.

After many treatments, the last stains of oil are finally removed from Papa's feathers and he looks nice and shiny again. Papa is grateful to have the stinking oil off his feathers because he senses the arrival of the autumn storms. Without his insulating black and white coat, he would never survive the biting frost.

A new day dawns and with it further change. The chicks have all shed their fluffy down and stand proudly in their black and white coats.

Dark clouds rush over the vast whiteness of Antarctica, now dotted by groups of busy people and their belongings. While the people seem unaware of the changing weather, all the penguins of the colony turn their backs toward the approaching storm. They lie down and wait.

The snowstorm hits the land with all its violent force.

For days on end the Antarctic is pounded by raging winds, which bring more and more snow in angry, horizontal sweeps.

When at last it is over, the land is transformed. Icebergs have been blown away and [new?]
ones have broken off the enormous glaciers. Everything is covered by a blanket of fresh sn[ow.]

Papa looks over his majestic homeland. There are no signs of the people anymore —
construction, barrels or garbage.

Could it be that they have gone?

Could it all have been a bad dream?

Or is there a world of ruins hidden under the gleaming snow . . . ?

To our children,
the future of this one and only earth . . .

For Janna, who was always there.

First published 1990
This paperback edition published 1992

Ashton Scholastic Ltd
Private Bag 1, Penrose, Auckland 5, New Zealand.

Ashton Scholastic Pty Ltd
PO Box 579, Gosford, NSW 2250, Australia.

Scholastic Inc.
730 Broadway, New York, NY 10003, USA.

Scholastic Canada Ltd
123 Newkirk Road, Richmond Hill, Ontario L4C 3G5, Canada.

Scholastic Publications Ltd
Marlborough House, Holly Walk, Leamington Spa, Warwickshire CV32 4LS,
England.

National Library of New Zealand
Cataloguing-in-Publication data

Glimmerveen, Ulco.
  A tale of Antarctica / by Ulco Glimmerveen. Auckland, N.Z. : Ashton
Scholastic, 1992, © 1989.
  1 v.
  Picture story book for children.
  ISBN 1-86943-091-3
  I. title.
  NZ823.2

8 7 6 5 4 3 2   5 6 7 8 9/9
Typeset in Century Old Style by Rennis Illustrations Ltd.